BUTLER AREA PUBLIC LIBRARY
BUTLER, PA.

GIVEN BY

Bucks for Books

Butler Area Public Library
218 North McKean Street
Butler PA 16001

Statistical Timeline and Overview of Gay Life

The Gallup's Guide to Modern Gay, Lesbian, & Transgender Lifestyle

BEING GAY, STAYING HEALTHY

**COMING OUT:
TELLING FAMILY AND FRIENDS**

**FEELING WRONG IN YOUR OWN BODY:
UNDERSTANDING WHAT IT MEANS TO BE TRANSGENDER**

GAY AND LESBIAN ROLE MODELS

**GAY BELIEVERS:
HOMOSEXUALITY AND RELIGION**

**GAY ISSUES AND POLITICS:
MARRIAGE, THE MILITARY, & WORK PLACE DISCRIMINATION**

**GAYS AND MENTAL HEALTH:
FIGHTING DEPRESSION, SAYING NO TO SUICIDE**

**HOMOPHOBIA:
FROM SOCIAL STIGMA TO HATE CRIMES**

**HOMOSEXUALITY AROUND THE WORLD:
SAFE HAVENS, CULTURAL CHALLENGES**

**A NEW GENERATION OF HOMOSEXUALITY:
MODERN TRENDS IN GAY & LESBIAN COMMUNITIES**

**SMASHING THE STEREOTYPES:
WHAT DOES IT MEAN TO BE GAY,
LESBIAN, BISEXUAL, OR TRANSGENDER?**

STATISTICAL TIMELINE AND OVERVIEW OF GAY LIFE

**WHAT CAUSES SEXUAL ORIENTATION?
GENETICS, BIOLOGY, PSYCHOLOGY**

**GAY PEOPLE OF COLOR:
FACING PREJUDICES, FORGING IDENTITIES**

**GAY CHARACTERS IN THEATER, MOVIES, AND TELEVISION:
NEW ROLES, NEW ATTITUDES**

Statistical Timeline and Overview of Gay Life

by Zachary Chastain

Mason Crest Publishers

Copyright © 2011 by Mason Crest Publishers. All rights reserved. No part of this publication may be reproduced or transmitted in any form or by any means, electronic or mechanical, including photocopying, recording, taping, or any information storage and retrieval system, without permission from the publisher.

MASON CREST PUBLISHERS INC.
370 Reed Road
Broomall, Pennsylvania 19008
(866)MCP-BOOK (toll free)
www.masoncrest.com

First Printing
9 8 7 6 5 4 3 2 1

Library of Congress Cataloging-in-Publication Data

Chastain, Zachary.
 Statistical timeline and overview of gay life / by Zachary Chastain.
    p. cm. -- (The Gallup's guide to modern gay, lesbian, & transgender lifestyle)
 Includes bibliographical references and index.
  ISBN 978-1-4222-1756-6 (hbk.)   ISBN 978-1-4222-1758-0   (series)
  ISBN 978-1-4222-1875-4 (pbk.)   ISBN 978-1-4222-1863-1 (pbk. series)
 1. Male homosexuality--History. 2. Lesbianism--History. 3. Gay men--History.
 4. Homosexuality--History. I. Title.
 HQ76.25.C44 2011
 306.76'609--dc22
                          2010026824

Produced by Harding House Publishing Service, Inc.
www.hardinghousepages.com
Interior design by MK Bassett-Harvey.
Cover design by Torque Advertising + Design.
Printed in the USA by Bang Printing.

Contents

INTRODUCTION 6
1. THE ANCIENT WORLD 9
2. THE MIDDLE AGES 21
3. A CHANGING WORLD 32
4. THE MODERN ERA 61
BIBLIOGRAPHY 88
INDEX 94
ABOUT THE AUTHOR AND THE CONSULTANT 96

PICTURE CREDITS

Berton, Ludovic; Creative Commons: p. 66
Bolognini, Stefano; Creative Commons: p. 72
Broadus, Lola: Creative Commons: p. 78
Centers for Disease Control and Prevention: p. 69
Creative Commons: pp. 10, 12, 14, 17, 18, 36, 44, 62, 77
Fox Searchlight Pictures: p. 42
Gallup: pp. 81, 82, 84, 86

Giabbanelli, Philippe; Creative Commons: p. 65
Legal Line: p. 78
Library of Congress: pp. 38, 47, 57
National Portrait Gallery of London: pp. 30, 50
Pixelcarpenter, Fotolia: p. 74
Turchenko, Vlad; Fotolia: p. 75
U.S. Holocaust Memorial Museum: p. 53

Introduction

We are both individuals and community members. Our differences define individuality; our commonalities create a community. Some differences, like the ability to run swiftly or to speak confidently, can make an individual stand out in a way that is viewed as beneficial by a community, while the group may frown upon others. Some of those differences may be difficult to hide (like skin color or physical disability), while others can be hidden (like religious views or sexual orientation). Moreover, what some communities or cultures deem as desirable differences, like thinness, is a negative quality in other contemporary communities. This is certainly the case with sexual orientation and gender identity, as explained in *Homosexuality Around the World*, one of the volumes in this book series.

Often, there is a tension between the individual (individual rights) and the community (common good). This is easily visible in everyday matters like the right to own land versus the common good of building roads. These cases sometimes result in community controversy and often are adjudicated by the courts.

An even more basic right than property ownership, however, is one's gender and sexuality. Does the right of gender expression trump the concerns and fears of a community or a family or a school? *Feeling Wrong in Your Own Body*, as the author of that volume suggests, means confronting, in the most personal way, the tension between individuality and community. And, while a community, family, and school have the right (and obligation) to protect its children, does the notion of property rights extend to controlling young adults' choice as to how they express themselves in terms of gender or sexuality?

Changes in how a community (or a majority of the community) thinks about an individual right or responsibility often precedes changes in the law enacted by legislatures or decided by courts. And for these changes to occur, individuals (sometimes working in small groups) often defied popular opinion, political pressure, or religious beliefs. Some of these trends are discussed in *A New Generation of Homosexuality*. Every generation (including yours!) stands on the accomplishments of our ancestors and in *Gay and Lesbian Role Models* you'll be reading about some of them.

One of the most pernicious aspects of discrimination on the basis of sexual orientation is that "homosexuality" is a stigma that can be hidden (see the volume about *Homophobia*). While some of my generation (I was your age in the early 1960s) think that life is so much easier being "queer" in the age of the Internet, Gay-Straight Alliances, and Ellen, in reality, being different in areas where difference matters is *always* difficult. Coming Out, as described in the volume of the same title, is always challenging—for both those who choose to come out and for the friends and family they trust with what was once a hidden truth. Being healthy means being honest—at least to yourself. Having supportive friends and family is most important, as explained in *Being Gay, Staying Healthy*.

Sometimes we create our own "families"—persons bound together by love and identity but not by name or bloodline. This is quite common in gay communities today as it was several generations ago. Forming families or small communities based on rejection by the larger community can also be a double-edged sword. While these can be positive, they may also turn into prisons of conformity. Does being lesbian, for example, mean everyone has short hair, hates men, and drives (or rides on) a motorcycle? *What Does It Mean to Be Gay, Lesbian, Bisexual, or Transgender?* "smashes" these and other stereotypes.

Another common misconception is that "all gay people are alike"—a classic example of a stereotypical statement. We may be drawn together because of a common prejudice or oppression, but we should not forfeit our individuality for the sake of the safety of a common identity, which is one of the challenges shown in *Gay People of Color: Facing Prejudices, Forging Identities*.

Coming out to who *you* are is just as important as having a group or "family" within which to safely come out. Becoming knowledgeable about these issues (through the books in this series and the other resources to which they will lead), feeling good about yourself, behaving safely, actively listening to others *and* to your inner spirit—all this will allow you to fulfill your promise and potential.

James T. Sears, PhD
Consultant

chapter 1

The Ancient World

Homosexuality has been around as long as the human race has. But the role of homosexuals in society has changed a great deal over the centuries.

The term "homosexuality" did not exist in the ancient world—but same-sex relationships did. People were not defined as homosexuals; instead, sexuality was seen as much more flexible, with people often having sexual relationships with both sexes. Gender was sometimes more fluid as well, with some individuals combining both male and female qualities into a single identity. The ancients apparently felt less of a need to categorize same-sex relationships as something that created a unique identity separated from "normal" or "straight" relationships. The boundary lines, if they even existed in the ancient world, were much more blurred.

As a result, discrimination and prejudice were not standard responses to homosexuals, as became the case later in history. Instead, these people were accepted, and sometimes even respected and honored. That changed in the Western world with the rise of the institutionalized Christian church.

Our journey through the history of homosexuality starts many centuries ago in long-ago Egypt. As we move forward through time, we gain a new understanding of this aspect of human life.

25th/24th Century BCE

Khnumhotep and Niankhkhnum's tomb was constructed in Egypt more than 4,000 years ago. In 1964, Ahmed Moussa discovered this tomb, which features illustrations of two men in a close embrace. It is not clear whether these two men were brothers, friends, or lovers, but

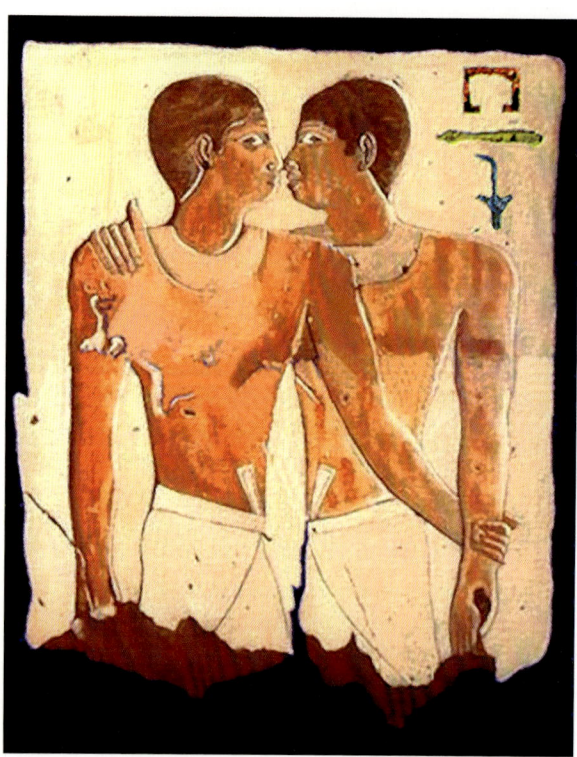

Khnumhotep and Niankhkhnum were the king's manicurists. Their portrait indicates that they may also have been gay.

EXTRA INFO

Homosexuality was an accepted behavior in ancient Africa and continued to be up until the arrival of Europeans on the continent. Women in Lesotho engaged in socially approved long-term relationships called motsoalle. Male Azande warriors in the northern Congo routinely took young male sexual mates between the ages of twelve and twenty, who helped their older husbands with household tasks.

some modern historians today have described Khnumhotep and Niankhkhnum as one of the earliest known gay relationships. They argue that the paintings on the wall of the tomb show the two in positions that are normally reserved for husband and wife pairs. However, the true relationship between these two manicurists to the king will never be known; other theories suggest that they were twins, suggesting another reason for their physical intimacy, as well as explaining the similarities in their names.

7th Century BCE

630–612 BCE

Sappho of Lesbos (an island in the Mediterranean Sea) is born. Sappho was one of the famous Greek poets and one of the first successful female poets. She is credited with inventing a unique type of metered poetry (now called sapphic meter) and changing how the poetry of the time was written; she wrote her poems to be accompanied by the music of a lyre and wrote from the first person, unlike many of the poets of her day. Much of her poetry deals with **homoerotic** images, which leads some scholars to suggest that

> **What's That Mean?**
>
> Something that is **homoerotic** refers to same-sex attraction and sexual behavior.

An ancient piece of pottery from the fifth century BCE provides an image of Sappho.

12 Statistical Timeline and Overview of Gay Life

relationships between women were not condemned then, as they would be in later centuries. Over time, Sappho's work became so connected with female eroticism that her life provided the terms "lesbian" and "sapphic," both of which are connected with gay women today. While her work has been hugely influential in the thousands of years since her death, only one of her poems exists in its entirety today.

I have not had one word from her.
Frankly I wish I were dead. When she left, she wept
a great deal; she said to me, "This parting must be
endured, Sappho. I go unwillingly."
I said, "Go, and be happy but remember (you know well)
whom you leave shackled by love.
"If you forget me, think of our gifts to Aphrodite and all
the loveliness that we shared
"all the violet tiaras, braided rosebuds, dill and crocus
twined around your young neck
"myrrh poured on your head and on soft mats girls with
all that they most wished for beside them
"while no voices chanted choruses without ours, no
woodlot bloomed in spring without song."
[Translated by Mary Barnard]

4th century BCE

385 BCE

Plato publishes the *Symposium*. This is a text that discusses the meaning and purpose of love; it takes the form, like many of Plato's texts, of a dialogue—in this case among a group of men who are together at a dinner party. The dialogue is not wholly about homosexual versus heterosexual love, but some of the men do mention **pederasty** and male-male erotic love. One character, a lawyer named Pausanius,

The Greek philosopher Plato discussed homosexual relationships. Such relationships were commonplace in ancient Greek society.

EXTRA INFO

Among native people of the ancient Americas prior to European colonization, a common form of same-sex sexuality centered around the Two-Spirit individual. Typically, this individual was recognized early in life, given a choice by the parents to follow the path, and, if the child accepted the role, raised in the appropriate manner, learning the customs of the gender it had chosen. Two-Spirit individuals were often shamans (holy people who communicated with the spirit world) and were revered as having powers beyond those of ordinary shamans. They usually took a sexual partner from among the ordinary tribe members of the same sex.

goes into great detail about the laws of consent for pederastic relationships in Greece at that time, while Aristophanes argues that all love is people's attempt to feel whole. He explains that at the time of creation, there were three genders: all male, all female, and androgynous (or half male and half female). However, at some point the androgynous beings tried to reach heaven and Zeus punished them by

What's That Mean?

Pederasty means "lover of boys." In Ancient Greece relationships between older men and male adolescents were common.

splitting them in half. So, all love is an attempt to get back to this wholeness—in some cases, this is attained by heterosexual relationships, while other times it is through homosexual eroticism that this feeling is found. Meanwhile, when it is Alcibiades' turn, he attempts to seduce Socrates himself and is

EXTRA INFO

In East Asia, same-sex love has been referred to since the earliest recorded history. Homosexuality in China, here the relationships were often marked by differences in age and social position, appears in written records as early as 600 BCE. Homosexuality in Japan, known as shudo or nanshoku, has been documented for over one thousand years and was an integral part of Buddhist monastic life and the samurai tradition; this same-sex love culture gave rise to strong traditions of painting and literature documenting and celebrating such relationships. Meanwhile, in Thailand, Kathoey or "ladyboys" have been a feature of Thai society for many centuries, and ancient Thai kings had male as well as female lovers. While Kathoey may encompass simple effeminacy or transvestism, Thai culture usually regards it as a third gender. These individuals are generally accepted by society, and Thailand has never had legal prohibitions against homosexuality or homosexual behavior.

A Renaissance portrayal of Socrates and Alcibiades.

ashamed when Socrates shows no interest. In the Symposium, homosexual relationships are treated as everyday and in a matter-of-fact manner. There are guidelines given for relationships, but these concern the mutual benefit of both parties involved rather than the gender or sex of the participants.

338 BCE

The Sacred Band of Thebes, an army made up of homosexual male couples, is defeated by Phillip II of Macedon. The Band consisted of 150 pairs of Greek male lovers, generally one older man, and a younger companion. The hope was that an army that consisted of men who were devoted to each other would

An ancient mosaic depicts the defeat of the Band of Thebes by Alexander the Great.

be more successful; that was indeed the case, and the Band remained undefeated for over thirty years. However, once Phillip II and his son Alexander the Great attacked Greece, the Band was defeated and most of them killed. They were buried in a communal grave, which was later excavated.

Third Century BCE

The Laws of Manu, the foundational work of Hindu law, mentions a "third sex," members of which may engage in nontraditional gender expression and homosexual activities. Historians are not sure exactly when this ancient book of law was written, only that it was sometime between 200 BCE and 200 CE.

First Century CE

54

Nero becomes the Emperor of Rome. Nero, like other Roman Emperors, took male lovers. However, he went even farther, marrying at least two men in legal wedding ceremonies.

218

One of the more extravagant and shocking Roman emperors, Elagabalus, begin his rule. He had at least one male spouse.

Fourth Century

314

The Council of Ancyra denies homosexuals the right to receive the Christian **sacrament**. This early Christian decree meant that anyone suspected of homosexuality could not be a full member of the Church. In 323, the Emperor Constantine converted to Christianity, making homosexuals' participation in the Church even harder.

342

The Roman Empire passes the first law against same-sex marriage. The Emperors Constantius II and Constans, the sons of Constantine, outlawed all homosexual marriages. This law began a tradition of increasing **discrimination** against homosexuals in the Roman Empire. However, there are rumors that Constans himself took several male lovers during his lifetime.

> **What's That Mean?**
>
> A **sacrament** is a religious ceremony with deep spiritual importance and meaning.
>
> **Discrimination** is the unfair treatment of a person or group, often backed up by law and custom.

chapter 2

The Middle Ages

During the Middle Ages, Christian **philosophers** distrusted the body's urges. They felt that sex in general led to sin, and the only sexual acts that were permitted were those that led to pregnancy. In other words, sex was allowed only for **procreation**, not for enjoyment and not for the expression of love between two people. This belief obviously ruled out many forms of heterosexual intercourse—and all homosexual relationships.

However, the men who preached this philosophy were **intellectuals** who often did not even move in the same

What's That Mean?

Philosophers are people who study moral and spiritual ideas in a search for a greater understanding of the meaning of life.

Procreation is the act of producing babies.

Intellectuals are people for whom the development of the mind, education, and study are the most important things in life.

> ## What's That Mean?
>
> **Theologians** are specialists in the study of God and God's relationship with the world.
>
> **Sodomy** is sexual behavior other than heterosexual intercourse, especially sex between men.

circles as ordinary people did. So while the Church spoke out against homosexuality, people continued to practice it.

Thirteenth Century

1225

St. Thomas Aquinas is born. Aquinas is considered one of the greatest Christian **theologians**; his ideas have greatly influenced Western thought. His views on homosexuality were definitely unfavorable. He believed that homosexuality is an unnatural characteristic, since it does not lead to the creation of children, like heterosexual relations do.

Fourteenth Century

1321

Dante Alighieri dies. Dante is the author of the Divine Comedy, which he worked on until his death. The Divine Comedy is an epic poem describing the worlds of the afterlife. In the first part, called Inferno, Dante presents the seven circles of hell. He places sodomites—those who commit **sodomy**—in the inner circle. The sinners in the seventh circle have committed crimes against God. Dante understands homosexuals to have rejected the natural order (the act of reproduction), created and directed by God.

Fifteenth Century

1470

Leonardo da Vinci is accused of sodomy. Da Vinci was a famous Italian Renaissance painter and inventor. An anonymous person accused da Vinci and three other men of sodomy with a seventeen-year-old model and male prostitute. Although he was jailed, he was freed

Some art historians have speculated that Mona Lisa, da Vinci's most famous painting, is actually a self-portrait of the great artist himself, expressing his ambivalent feelings about his sexual identity.

because of lack of evidence. There is strong support for da Vinci's homosexuality, although it was never proved in a court of law. He never took a wife, or had any known relationships with women, although he did have many close friendships with men. His art often depicts masculanized beauty (the Mona Lisa is a famous example) and masculine sexuality.

This drawing shows two male lovers being burned at the stake outside Zürich in 1482. Despite incidents like this, historians have recently discovered that a form of male same-sex marriage existed in medieval France, and possibly other areas in Europe as well.

EXTRA INFO

During the Renaissance, wealthy cities in northern Italy—Florence and Venice in particular—were known for their widespread practice of same-sex love, engaged in by a considerable part of the male population. As common and socially acceptable as the practice was, however, the authorities—known as the Officers of the Night Court—were prosecuting, fining, and imprisoning a good portion of that population for these acts.

Sixteenth Century

1501

In Persia (modern-day Iran), homosexuality and homoerotic expressions are tolerated in numerous public places, from monasteries and seminaries to taverns, military camps, bathhouses, and coffee houses. For the next two hundred years in Persia, male houses of prostitution will be legally recognized and pay taxes.

1513

The first European explorers arrive in Mexico and South America, and are horrified to find the native people openly practicing same-sex relationships. Balboa sets his dogs on native people practicing "male love," and in the years that follow, the **conquistadors** try to wipe out the practice by subjecting anyone they find engaging in same-sex relationships to severe penalties, including public execution, burning, and being torn to pieces by dogs.

What's That Mean?

The *conquistadors* were military men from Spain who explored and conquered Mexico and South America.

1533

King Henry VIII of England passes the Buggery Act of 1533. Famous for his six wives, Henry VIII was not as accommodating of homosexuals. The Buggery Act made sodomy punishable by death by hanging. (Buggery is a British term for sodomy.) This was England's first legislation concerned with homosexuality; before that it was considered immoral, but not criminal. The act would not be repealed until 1861, over three hundred years later.

1570

An estimated 1,000 cases of sodomy are tried by the Spanish Inquisition between 1570 and 1630. The Inquisition was created in 1478 to root out religious

Henry VIII had issues with sexuality. Unable to control his own sexual desires for the good of his realm, he also put in place the first legal persecution of homosexuals in England.

heresy and other socially ***deviant*** behavior in Spain. It was known for its unfair trials and brutal methods of torture and execution. The Inquisition eventually expanded to homosexuality, mostly persecuting men but a handful of women too. The Portuguese Inquisition, inspired by the one in Spain, was set up in 1536 and tried 500 sodomy cases by the end of its run.

The Inquisition was an early example of the organized church acting in a way that was the exact opposite of Christ's teachings on love.

Seventeenth Century

1603

James I becomes king of England; he has an openly homosexual relationship with the Duke of Buckingham.

1624

Richard Cornish is the first person to be executed in America for homosexuality. Cornish was the captain of the ship *Ambrose*. He was accused of luring a cabin boy into his room to commit homosexual acts while the ship was anchored in the James River in Virginia. He was found guilty and later hanged. A year later, Cornish's brother asserted his innocence, but was unable to clear his name.

> **What's That Mean?**
>
> **Heresy** is religious belief or opinion that goes against an established religious authority.
>
> **Deviant** means behavior that is judged to be negative and against the accepted rules of society

1649

The first criminal conviction of lesbianism takes place in North America. In Plymouth, Massachusetts, Sarah White Norman was charged with having

King James I was responsible for the publication of the most famous English translation of the Bible. Although he was married and fathered children, historians speculate that he may have also been homosexual.

homosexual relations with Mary Vincent Hammon, then sixteen. Norman was prosecuted, but Hammon was not because of her age.

1655

The town of New Haven, now in Connecticut, passes the only colonial American law against women's homosexual behavior. The law authorized the death penalty for sodomy, as well as lesbianism. However, it's unlikely that the law was ever actually used against a woman. Previously, Connecticut had a history of reacting strongly to homosexuality. The original charter that set out the governance of the British colony stated that its laws had to be the same as in England. This meant that homosexuality was a crime punishable by the death sentence for men. Several sodomy cases were tried in the colony, which resulted in at least two hangings.

chapter 3

A Changing World

In the 1700s, life became much more difficult for gay men in Europe and America. Up until then, many men had been able to avoid much of the public abuse and severe penalties given to convicted "sodomites" of the lower class, but now, only extreme wealth could save them from public disapproval and consequences. Groups dedicated to the preservation of public morals would often arrest openly gay men through spying and entrapment. This forced gays to go underground and resort to more discreet locations for their encounters. Gentlemen resigned themselves to keeping to the privacy of their homes, engaging in often well-known and highly complex relationships among themselves. Working-class gay men had "molly" houses, places where gay men could meet to socialize, meet for sex, or cross-dress in a relatively safe place with like-minded companions.

Meanwhile, all over Europe, the eighteenth century was a time when cross-dressing women became more common. Posing as men increased women's ability to enjoy a greater degree of financial and social freedom. It also allowed lower-class women, who didn't have the same privileges of the relatively **permissive** upper classes, a way to practice lesbianism without being noticed. Women who were prosecuted for posing as men often had wives. Upon discovery of these

> **What's That Mean?**
>
> Something that is *permissive* allows for a wide range of behavior without strict moral judgement.

Englishwoman Hannah Snell served as a man in the Royal Marines for four years in the 18th century. She assumed the identity of her brother-in-law after her husband deserted her.

unions, courts were predictably harder on the "male" partner, viewing their wives as innocent victims.

The nineteenth century brought new attitudes toward homosexuality in Europe and America. Until this era, gays and lesbians had not been viewed as people who were homosexual, but as people who happened to engage in sexual acts with members of their own gender. In other words, homosexuality was something a person did, not something a person was. At this point in history, many people believed that individuals consciously chose to perform homosexual acts, and consequently, homosexuality was considered a crime—in some cases, punishable by death—in some nations. Between 1800 and 1834, eighty men were hung in Great Britain for committing sodomy.

In the twentieth century, medical and psychological experts began to claim that people who engaged in same-sex act suffered from a disease or "psychological deviancy," and homosexuality became associated with insanity. However, it was also still considered a crime.

Eighteenth Century

1779

Thomas Jefferson proposes a criminal law dealing with sodomy in Virginia. Before the end of the

American Revolutionary War, Virginia lawmakers began drafting a legal code to be ready for American victory against the British. Among other laws, Jefferson prepared a criminal law that would outlaw the death penalty for cases of sodomy. However, it instead called for castration in the case of men who were convicted of sodomy. For women, the law required that a hole would be bored into the cartilage of the nose, at least a half inch in diameter.

1791

France becomes the first country to adopt a **penal code** that does not **criminalize** sodomy. Two years earlier, the National Constituent Assembly met to reform French government and law. Along with sodomy, the assembly decriminalized any private actions that had to do with superstition or religion, including witchcraft, **incest**, and **sacrilege**. Including sodomy among the list of decriminalized acts was a first step in promoting homosexual

> **What's That Mean?**
>
> A *penal code* is a government's official rules regarding crime and its appropriate legal punishment.
>
> To *criminalize* something is to make it illegal.
>
> *Incest* refers to sexual behavior between people who are closely related.
>
> *Sacrilege* is an act of disrespect against something considered holy.

A Changing World

rights in Europe and the world, but did not eliminate persecution or discrimination against them.

Nineteenth Century

1830

Brazil decriminalizes homosexuality. Dom Pedro I, the Portuguese emperor of Brazil, signed the Imperial Penal Code, which eliminated sodomy from criminal

The National Constituent Assembly in 1791 reformed the French government and decriminalized homosexuality.

acts. In modern-day Brazil, several state constitutions and municipal statutes have made discrimination illegal if it was based on sexuality.

1832

Russia criminalizes homosexuality. Article 995 established male homosexual acts as criminal; any man convicted under the act could be sent to Siberia for up to five years of exile. The law was rarely enforced, and many prominent Russian artists were known for their homosexual tendencies. Tolerance of homosexuality increased throughout the next century, but was suppressed under Soviet Russia. It wasn't fully decriminalized until another law, Article 121, was signed in 1993, almost two hundred years after the first law was put in place.

1834

James Buchanan, later President of the United States, meets William Rufus De Van King, who becomes his nearly inseparable companion for almost a decade. Buchanan and King's relationship is well-known in political circles, with Andrew Jackson referring to King as "Miss Nancy" and others calling King "Buchanan's better half."

Whitman's biographers continue to debate his sexuality, but he is usually described as having been either homosexual or bisexual in his feelings and attractions.

1836

The last reported execution for homosexuality takes place in Great Britain. Though there were no more executions after this year, it wasn't until 1861 that the death penalty for sodomy was actually removed from the British law code. The Offences Against the Person Act of 1861 officially removed the death sentence for "buggery." The Act established imprisonment from ten years to life as a replacement for the death penalty.

> **What's That Mean?**
>
> To *repeal* a law is to vote to make it no longer in effect.

1860

American poet Walt Whitman publishes *Leaves of Grass*, which includes numerous references to comradely love between men.

1867

Karl Heinrich Ulrichs becomes the first homosexual to speak out publicly for gay rights. On August 29, Ulrichs urged the Congress of German Jurists in Munich, Germany, to *repeal* anti-homosexual laws; he was not successful. Karl Ulrichs was a lawyer and journalist, as well as a tireless supporter of homosexuals, and wrote twelve pamphlets titled "Researches into the Riddle of Love Between Men." He also tried to start a publication for homosexuals, but he only published one issue because of lack of support for his venture.

1870

The first American novel about homosexuality is published. While he never mentions homosexuality **explicitly,** author Bayard Taylor explores themes of homosexual love between two men in *Joseph and His Friend: A Story of Pennsylvania*. Literature that hints at homosexual behavior and relationships had already been published in Europe, including works by Lord Byron and Alfred, Lord Tennyson. However, Taylor's novel is possibly the first to appear in the United States.

> ### What's That Mean?
>
> **Explicitly** means openly, and in detail.
>
> A **brothel** is a "house of prostitution," a place where prostitutes entertain their customers.

1889

The Cleveland Street Scandal becomes big news in England. In July, the London police were sent to a male brothel on Cleveland Street, intending to arrest Charles Hammond and a teenage accomplice named Henry Newlove. Hammond had fled, but they eventually found and arrested Newlove, who identified several prominent persons as customers of the brothel, including noblemen and the Queen's grandson. Although the **brothel** closing was relatively boring news, a newspaper editor picked up on it and spread the rumor of a cover-up. He wondered why those convicted got off so lightly (none got the usual two-year sentences for homosexual acts), and why the noblemen were not arrested. The editor never proved his theory, but he did end up in jail for making false accusations of one of the earls rumored to be involved in the scandal.

The poet Lord Byron was known for his love affairs—with both women and men.

1892

The English use of the word homosexual is first recorded, along with bisexual and heterosexual. In the same year, the American Charles Gilbert Chaddock translated Richard von Krafft-Ebbing's book, Psychopathia Sexualis, from German into English. The word homosexual comes from the Greek homo, meaning "same," and the Latin sex.

Alfred Kinsey's life—and research on sexual behaviors—were portrayed in the 2004 movie Kinsey.

Author Oscar Wilde spent time in prison because of his homosexuality.

1894

Alfred Kinsey is born on June 23. Kinsey was a biologist and psychologist, and one of the first Americans to research human sexuality. He conducted his research at Indiana University in the 1930s and 1940s, mainly collecting thousands of interviews with people discussing their sexual experiences. He published *Sexual Behavior in the Human Male* in 1948, followed by *Sexual Behavior in the Human Female* in 1953. His life and research is the basis for the 2004 movie called *Kinsey*.

The first group with the political aim of fighting homosexual persecution is formed. Prominent

A Changing World 43

among the members of the group called Cercle Hermaphroditos is Earl Lind. Lind was born a Puritan in Connecticut. He eventually moves to New York City and discovers the homosexual underground, inspiring him to write several books later in life.

Irish author Oscar Wilde goes on trial for homosexuality. Accused by his male lover's father of sodomy, Wilde is sent to trial in London. His writing, including *The Picture of Dorian Gray*, is used as proof that he has committed homosexual acts. He is convicted and sentenced to two years of hard labor. At this point, homosexuality is not punishable by death, but it is still a criminal act that could lead to imprisonment.

1897

The homosexual rights organization movement gets its start in Germany. Dr. Magnus Hirschfeld organizes the Scientific Humanitarian Committee, urging fellow homosexuals as well as celebrities to support his movement and homosexual rights in general. Hirschfeld is a Jewish medical doctor interested in human sexuality, and claims to be a transvestite as well as a homosexual. He succeeds in speaking to thousands of people during his lifetime, and convinces many of the need to be open about sexuality. All traces of the movement are eventually wiped out by the German Nazis in the 1930s.

20th Century

1903

In New York City on February 21st, 1903, New York police carry out what has come to be known as the first raid on a gay bathhouse in the history of the United States. The bathhouse is called the Ariston Hotel Baths. During the raid, police arrest twenty-six homosexual men. Of these twenty-six men, twelve are brought to trial on criminal charges of sodomy. As a result of the police raid, seven men arrested at the Ariston Hotel Baths are sentenced to time in prison, ranging from four to as many as twenty years.

Magnus Hirschfeld did his best to educate his society about homosexuality.

1906

Imre: A Memorandum, widely considered one of the first openly gay novels to be published in the United States, is written and released by Edward Irenaeus Prime-Stevenson. Published under the pseudonym Xavier Mayne, the novel is given an initial print run of just 500 copies. *Imre*'s story centers around a relationship between two men who meet by chance in Budapest.

1907–1909

The Harden-Eulenburg Affair, sometimes called the Eulenberg Affair, is unfolding in Germany. After accusations of homosexual conduct between members of Kaiser Wilhelm II's cabinet and close advisers surface, several trials and court-marshals provide the first widespread public discussion of homosexuality in Germany, though in the context of a major political scandal.

What's That Mean?

An *anarchist* is someone who rebels against power and authority.

A *social activist* is someone who works for change in the political, economic, and legal system in order to improve people's lives

1910

Emma Goldman, a Russian emigrant living in New York City, begins speaking out in favor of the rights of homosexuals in public. Goldman was known as an **anarchist** and ***social activist***. She regularly championed women's rights and was arrested for "inciting to riot" and illegally distributing informational material about birth control. Magnus Hirschfield wrote of Goldman, "She was the first and only woman, indeed the first and only American, to take up the defense of homosexual love before the general public."

1913

The word "faggot" is first used in print to refer to homosexual men, appearing in a vocabulary of crim-

Emma Goldman's writing and lectures spanned a wide variety of issues, including prisons, freedom of speech, and homosexuality.

inal slang published in Portland, Oregon. In the text, the word is explained as a synonym for "sissies."

1917

The October Revolution in Russia (which would later result in the creation of the Soviet Union) repeals the Russian criminal code entirely, rewriting it over the course of the next several years. When the new code is completed, it lacks any mention of homosexuality, specifically outlawed in Article 995 of the old criminal code.

1920

Subculture groups begin to use the word "gay" in reference to homosexuality and homosexuals themselves.

1923

The word "fag" is first used in print to refer to homosexuals. Nels Anderson's *The Hobo* features the sentence: "Fairies or Fags are men or boys who exploit sex for profit." A **sociologist**, Anderson, wrote *The Hobo* in order to shed light on the plight of Chicago's homeless poor.

What's That Mean?

A *subculture* is a group of people who share a lifestyle that is different and separate from the larger majority.

A *sociologist* is a scientist who studies how people, institutions, and communities interact in society.

EXTRA INFO

In many societies of Melanesia, especially in Papua New Guinea, same-sex relationships were an integral part of the culture until the middle of the twentieth century. The Etoro and Marind-anim people, for example, even viewed heterosexuality as sinful and celebrated homosexuality instead. Many Melanesian societies, however, have become hostile towards same-sex relationships since the introduction of Christianity by European missionaries.

1926

The word "homosexuality" first appears in the *New York Times*, making the newspaper the first major publication to print it.

1927

Around this time, the Pansy Craze is taking hold in underground culture. During the late 1920s and early 1930s, gay clubs and performers (called "pansy" performers) become popular in the United States. Laws against public displays of gay behavior closes many of these clubs down.

1928

Author Radclyffe Hall's *The Well of Loneliness* is first published in the United Kingdom, and then later in the United States. The novel's protagonist, Stephen Gordon, is an upper-class English woman who finds love with another woman, though they are kept apart by social rejection and isolation. In *The Well of Loneliness*, Hall uses the phrase "sexual **inversion**" to refer to Gordon's homosexuality. Born Marguerite Radclyffe-Hall, Hall described herself as an "***invert***" as well. In her novel, homosexuality is portrayed as normal and natural, and Hall makes a point of pleading for acceptance of homosexuals by writing, "Give us the right to our existence." *The Well of Loneliness*

Author Radclyffe Hall was openly lesbian. In her twenties, her long-time lover gave her the nickname "John," which she went by for the rest of her life.

is Hall's best-known novel; though she had written several before it and would go on to write several after it had been published, including the highly regarded *Adam's Breed*.

At the time it is published, *The Well of Loneliness* becomes the target of a public campaign led by James Douglas, editor of the *Sunday Express*, a British newspaper. Though the book does not feature any explicit material, it is deemed to be obscene in British courts because of its defense of what the judge calls "unnatural practices between women." U.S. courts rule in favor of *The Well of Loneliness*, allowing its publication in the States. The **controversy** surrounding the book drives public discussion, and increased public visibility, of gay women in both Britain and the United States.

What's That Mean?

Inversion is a reversal, the opposite, of what is considered usual.

An **invert** is someone whose sexual attraction is "reversed," and an early-20th century term for a gay person.

A **controversy** is an issue that creates strong opinions on all sides.

1933

The National Socialist German Workers Party (known as the Nazi Party) bans all homosexual groups. The Nazis begin to round up homosexuals and send them to concentration camps. In addition, they destroy Magnus Hirschfeld's Institute for Sexual Research, burning the Institute's library.

In Denmark and the Philippines, homosexuality is decriminalized, with all laws prohibiting it taken off the books.

In the Soviet Union (the U.S.S.R.), homosexual acts are once again made criminal. Laws prohibiting homosexual sex had not existed since the time of the October Revolution in 1917, when laws disallowing "a man from laying with another man" were removed from Russia's criminal code.

1937

The Nazis begin using pink triangles to identify homosexual men. Gay men are forced to wear the triangle on their clothing at all times so that they may be easily identified in concentration camps.

1942

Switzerland removes all laws prohibiting homosexuality from its criminal code.

1945

After Allied soldiers liberate the concentration camps in which the Nazis imprisoned and killed Jews, gypsies, and homosexuals (among others), gay prisoners are not set free. Instead, they are made to serve out

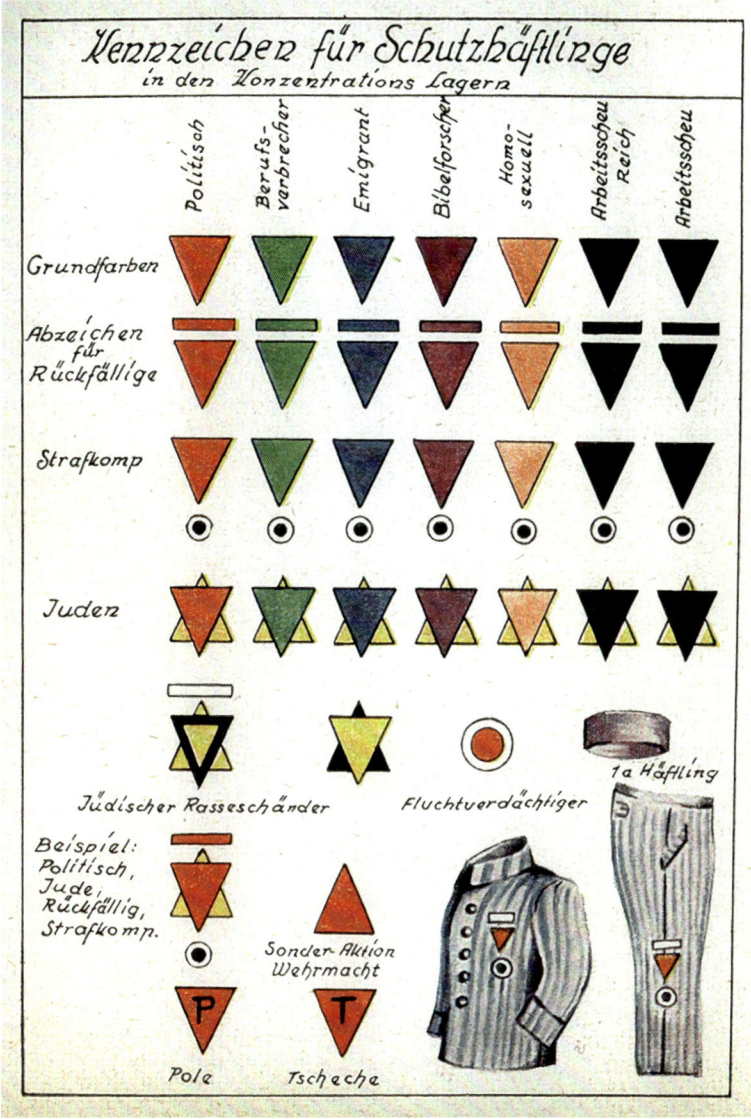

A chart of prisoner markings used in German concentration camps. The vertical categories list markings for the following types of prisoners: political, professional criminal, emigrant, Jehovah's Witnesses, homosexual, Germans shy of work, and other nationalities shy of work. The horizontal categories begin with the basic colors, and then show those for repeat offenders and for those who were also Jewish.

the remainder of their prison sentences under a section of Germany's criminal code that outlaws homosexual acts between men. Called Paragraph 175, the law had been on the books since 1871, though its expansion under Nazi rule allowed for the wide scale imprisonment of homosexuals in concentration camps. The law would not be removed from Germany's criminal code entirely until 1994, after numerous revisions over the course of more than a century.

Four gay veterans form the Veterans Benevolent Association (VBA), the first veterans' group dedicated to gay issues. Founded in New York City, VBA served as both a social group, but also as a way to express anger about the military's policy of giving "blue discharges" to gay servicemen. Blue discharges meant that a soldier's service would end, and that their discharge was less-than-honorable (though, importantly, not dishonorable). The Veterans Benevolent Association partnered with NAACP to advocate for the end of blue discharges, also given in ***dispropor-***

> **What's That Mean?**
>
> ***Disproportionate*** means in unfair and unequal numbers.
>
> ***LGBT*** refers to people who are lesbian, gay, bisexual, or transgender; it is an all-inclusive term used for this community of people.
>
> ***Advocacy*** means the public support of a social or political cause.

tionate numbers to African-American servicemen. The VBA would disband in 1954, when several members would go on to found other **LGBT** organizations.

1946

The Center for Culture and Recreation (also known by the Dutch acronym COC) is formed in the Netherlands. COC is one of the first pro-gay rights organizations in the world. A key part of the homophile movement of the 1950s and '60s (the name given to all gay rights ***advocacy*** at the time), COC is one of the longest lasting LGBT organizations ever founded.

1947

Lisa Ben self-publishes *Vice Versa*, the first LGBT magazine to be released in North America. Started in Los Angeles, *Vice Versa* was created mostly while Ben was at work as a secretary in a movie studio. Ben, whose pen name "Lisa Ben" was an anagram of the word "lesbian" (she was born Edith Eyde) published nine issues of *Vice Versa*.

1950

The Organization for Sexual Equality is founded in Sweden. The organization still exists today, under the name Swedish Federation for Lesbian, Gay, Bisexual and Transgender Rights (RFSL).

> **What's That Mean?**
>
> **Civil rights** refers to rights and freedoms that protect people from unfair treatment by those in authority.

East Germany alters Paragraph 175, the section of Germany's criminal code that prohibited homosexual acts, rolling back many of the changes that the Nazis had introduced. The law was rewritten to be closer to the pre-1935 version of the law, though some language from the Nazi party's version of Paragraph 175 remained.

The Mattachine Society, one of the first American organizations devoted to LGBT rights, is formed in Los Angeles on November 11. Initially, founders of the group use the structure of the Communist Party as a model for their organization. Later, the Mattachine Society would adopt a structure more similar to other *civil rights* groups.

Senator Joseph McCarthy claims that a "homosexual underground" has developed in the U.S. State Department. One hundred ninety gay government workers are dismissed from their jobs because of their sexual orientation as a result of McCarthy's claims. The firing of these workers marks the start of what has come to be known as the Lavender Scare, a period during which homosexuals feared persecution, much in the same way McCarthy's Red Scare targeted people for their political affiliations.

Joseph McCarthy was a worried man. Two of the things that apparently worried him most were communism and homosexuality.

Christine Jorgensen became a spokesperson for transsexual and transgender people.

1952

Christine Jorgensen is the first person to undergo sex reassignment surgery widely known about by the public. After the surgery, in which Jorgensen became a woman, she became something of a celebrity, appearing on television talk shows and in newspaper stories.

1956

The nation of Thailand eliminates laws on its books that criminalize sex between members of the same gender.

1957

The Wolfenden Committee submits its report (Report of the Departmental Committee on Homosexual Offences and Prostitution) recommending that laws that make homosexual acts between consenting adults criminal should be removed from Britain's criminal code. The committee, named after its chairman, Lord Wolfenden, was created after several famous men were convicted for having committed homosexual acts.

Psychologist Evelyn Hooker publishes a study that shows homosexual men are just as well adjusted as men who are not gay. Her study is seen today as vital to the 1973 decision by the American Psychiatric Association to remove homosexuality from its guide to mental disorders, the Diagnostic and Statistical Manual of Mental Disorders (DSM).

What's That Mean?

The **First Amendment** of the U.S. Constitution protects such basic rights as the freedom of speech, the freedom of the press, and freedom of religion.

1958

The U.S. Supreme Court rules in favor of the **First Amendment** rights of a magazine devoted to gay and lesbian issues. This is the first time the Supreme Court ruled on a case that specifically addressed homosexuality.

chapter 4

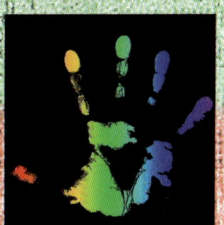

The Modern Era

History has seen many changes in the way homosexuality is regarded. It has been condoned and condemned, accepted and discriminated against, honored and hated. The pendulum has swung back and forth.

Nowadays, gay rights are openly discussed and advocated. At the same time, they have not yet been fully achieved, and homophobia is unfortunately still alive and well.

1961

The Roman Catholic Church declares that those "affected by the *perverse inclination*" of homosexuality should be prohibited from taking religious vows or be ordained. This declaration specifically forbids any homosexual members of the priesthood.

What's That Mean?

Something that is *perverse* is against the accepted moral standard, especially in matters of sexual behavior.

An *inclination* is an attraction toward a particular choice.

In San Francisco, José Sarria becomes the first openly gay candidate for office to run in the United States. Sarria campaigns for a position on the San Francisco Board of Supervisors.

1961

Illinois becomes the first state in the Union to remove all laws prohibiting sodomy from state criminal code. This change would take effect in 1962.

1966

The Mattachine Society holds what it calls a "Sip-In" at New York City's Julius Bar. The action is staged to

Christopher Park in New York City, where many of the demonstrators met after the Stonewall riots to talk about what had happened, now features a sculpture of four white figures by George Segal that commemorates the milestone in gay history.

protest a New York State Liquor Authority keeping alcohol from being served to homosexuals. Founded in the 1950s, the Mattachine Society is considered one of the first American gay rights groups.

1969

The Stonewall Riots occur in New York City. The police raid the Stonewall Inn, a popular gay bar. This happened often in various bars around the city, but on this particular night, June 28, the customers fight back. A crowd gathers in the street outside the bar and fights with police. The crowd continues to grow, until a riot-control team is finally able to disperse them. The next night, thousands of gay people swarmed the streets, in the name of Gay Pride, again getting into conflict with the police. Riots continued throughout the week. The Stonewall Riots are considered the birth of the modern gay rights movement and are remembered with Gay Pride events in the month of June all over the world.

Canada legalized homosexual behavior. Prior to this, homosexuality was punishable by up to fourteen years in prison; the new law made **consensual** acts involving adults over twenty-one years of age legal.

> **What's That Mean?**
>
> Something that is **consensual** is done willingly by the people involved.

The Modern Era 63

1970

The first gay pride march takes place in New York City. Thousands of people marched from Greenwich Village to Central Park in remembrance of the Stonewall Riots. Chicago, San Francisco, and Los Angeles also started holding pride events at this time, events which still happen annually to this day.

The University of Michigan establishes the "Gay Advocate's Office" at its Ann Arbor campus.

1971

Idaho repeals its sodomy law, becoming the third state in the nation to legalize consensual male homosexual behavior. However, Mormon and Catholic officials—two large groups in Idaho—did not agree with this position, and the law was reinstated in April of 1972.

1972

Sweden becomes the first country in the world to allow its citizens to legally change their sex and even helps by providing free hormone therapy.

1973

The American Psychiatric Association (APA) removes homosexuality from its Diagnostic and Statistical Manual of Mental Disorders (DSM-II). However, it wasn't until 1994, twenty-one years later, that the APA

Gay Pride Parades would become annual events in countries all around the world.

The Modern Era 65

released a statement saying that, "Homosexuality is neither a mental illness nor a moral depravity. It is the way a portion of the population expresses human love and sexuality."

1977

Harvey Milk is elected supervisor in San Francisco, on his third try for office. He was one of the first openly gay people elected to public office in the United States. Throughout his campaign and term as supervisor, Milk stressed the importance of the

The Rainbow Flag has become a symbol of gay pride and identity.

government's care for the community, the support of gay rights, and the preservation of San Francisco's neighborhoods. He fought to pass a law that prohibited discrimination based on sexual orientation, and was responsible for the city's hiring of more LGBT police officers and the state's refusal to prohibit gays and lesbians from teaching in public schools.

1978

> **What's That Mean?**
>
> *Impaired* means not operating or behaving normally.

The rainbow flag was developed as a sign for LGBT pride. Harvey Milk decided that the Gay Freedom Day Parade needed a visual symbol. So he talked to his friend, Gilbert Baker, who designed the flag that is now synonymous with gay rights.

On November 27, Harvey Milk is assassinated. He is shot by Dan White, a city supervisor who had quit after San Francisco had passed a gay rights law. During the resulting trial, White's lawyers argued that White's judgment was *impaired* because he had eaten too much junk food; this defense worked, and White served only five years for voluntary manslaughter instead of being convicted for first degree murder. This light sentence (and slightly outrageous defense) angered the LGBT community all over the country; riots broke out in San Francisco as a response. Since his assassination, Milk has become a symbol of gay rights in the United States.

1979

The first National March on Washington for Lesbian and Gay Rights is held on October 14. It was timed to coincide with the tenth anniversary of the Stonewall Riots, with more than 100,000 people participating from across the country and the world.

1980

The Democratic Part runs on a gay-rights plank as part of its platform. This was the point at which political parties realized that the LGBT community had a tremendous amount of voting power. This was the first attempt to try and appeal to that community.

1981

The first cases of AIDS are documented (although there is no way of telling if the disease was present in some form before this date). Eight young, gay men in New York City were diagnosed with Kaposi's Sarcoma, a rare form of cancer that normally occurs in older people. At the same time, a rare form of pneumonia was diagnosed in both New York and California, also mainly among gay men. In June, the CDC founded a task force on Kaposi's Sarcoma and Opportunistic Infections, seeking to discover why all these rare *infectious diseases* were spreading. This was the beginning of AIDS awareness in the United States, but no one knew how the disease was spread or what was causing it.

More than half of transsexual youths surveyed are found to have attempted suicide.

What's That Mean?

An *infectious disease* is one that can be spread by germs.

1982

AIDS continues to spread, although it still does not have a name. At this point, the CDC referred to it by the names of the diseases that it caused. There

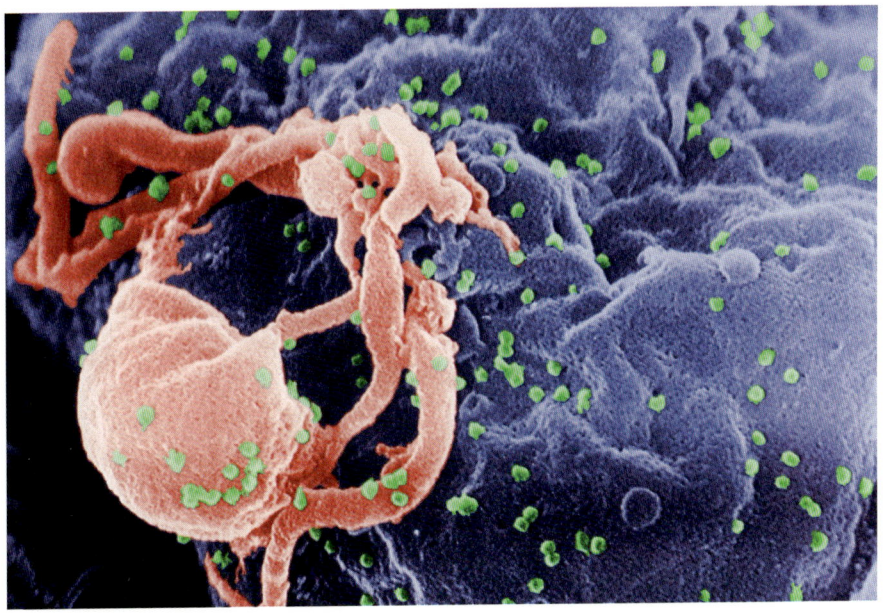

The virus that changed the world.

The Modern Era 69

This memorial is in Berlin for the homosexual victims of the Holocaust. Its inscription reads (in German) "Struck Dead— Hushed Up."

was still no consensus about how the disease was spread, but some people linked it to its **prevalence** among gay men, calling it GRID (gay-related immune deficiency), "gay cancer," or "community-acquired immune dysfunction." By the beginning of July 1982, there were more than 452 cases, and reports began to come in of the disease among Haitians and hemophiliacs, as well as gay men. In September, the CDC finally settles on a name: AIDS, or Acquired Immune Deficiency Syndrome.

> **What's That Mean?**
>
> **Prevalence** is the number of times that something occurs, how common or uncommon it is.

1984

The first memorial to gay Holocaust victims appears in the former concentration camp of Mauthausen. Since then, other concentration camps have built their own monuments; often times other survivor groups object to these memorials, which is why they were not erected until the mid-1980s.

1987

Twenty-eight percent of gay and lesbian high school students in a U.S. study were found to have dropped

The Modern Era

out of school because of **harassment** resulting from their sexual orientation.

Eighty percent of lesbians, gay, and bisexual youth reported severe isolation problems. They experienced social isolation, emotional isolation, and **cognitive isolation.**

A study finds that 26 percent of American gays and lesbian youth are forced to leave home because of conflicts with their families over their sexual identities.

The U.S. Department of Justice reports that homosexuals are the most frequent victims of hate crimes.

A gay pride parade in Copenhagen in 2008. Denmark has a liberal stance toward same-sex couples.

1989

Denmark became the first country to pass a law allowing civil unions for same-sex couples, partnerships that had most of the same legal rights as heterosexual marriages. The law was called the Danish Registered Partnership Act.

A study finds that gay and lesbian youth are two to three times more likely to commit suicide than other youths, and 30 percent of all completed youth suicides are related to the issue of sexual identity. Suicide was the leading cause of death among gay, lesbian, bisexual, and transgendered youth.

> **What's That Mean?**
>
> **Harassment** means targeting a person or a group for bullying, violence, and unfair treatment.
>
> **Cognitive isolation** means a lack of access to information that could be important to your sense of self.

1990

In a study of depression and gay youth, researchers found depression strikes homosexual youth four to five times more severely than other non-gay peers.

The 1990 U.S. Census found that the seven largest concentrations of the lesbian and gay population in the United States are:

Being gay does not cause depression—but not being accepted by their communities, families, and faiths can make people depressed.

Manhattan
San Francisco
Boston/Cambridge
Seattle
Oakland/Berkeley
Washington, D.C.
Chicago/Evanston

Of all lesbians and gay men, 45.1 percent and 52.7 percent live in urban areas, respectively, while 33.1 percent and 31.7 percent live in the suburbs, respectively.

San Francisco is famous both for its cable cars and its acceptance of homosexuality.

The average household income for lesbians in the United States is estimated at $45,927, while for gay men it was $51,325. In 1990 the average household income in the U.S. for all families was $36,520.

1992

A survey of American gays and lesbians found that 55.5 percent of adult gay men and 71.2 percent of adult lesbians were in steady relationships.

In the five major U.S. cities that have professionally staffed agencies that monitor anti-lesbian and antigay violence—Boston, Chicago, Minneapolis and St. Paul, New York, and San Francisco—reports of anti-gay and anti-lesbian incidents increased by 172 percent in the five years since 1988.

The most common perpetrators of anti-lesbian and anti-gay violence—responsible for 50 percent of all reported incidents—are youths twenty-one or under; 94 percent of the perpetrators are male. About two-thirds of the perpetrators are unknown to the victims. Eighty-nine percent of all incidents reported to the New York City Anti-Violence Project in 1992 resulted in no arrest.

1993

Teena Brandon is murdered in Nebraska. Brandon was born female, but identified with the male gender. Throughout high school, he lived as a man, going by

Brandon Teena's life was short and tragic because of transgender prejudice.

Throughout high school, he lived as a man, going by the name Billy or Brandon instead of Teena, his birth name. He dated many girls, including Lisa Lambert. When Lambert and Brandon's friends found out that he was biologically female, they raped him and then shot both him and Lambert.

At about the same time, Minnesota passed the first state law that protected transgendered people from discrimination. The state expanded the definition of sexual orientation to include having a gender identity that is not associated with one's biological sex. However, the law also stated that employers could require employees to use restroom facilities that corresponded to their biological sex—the only way for a transgendered person to legally use the restroom of

The Modern Era 77

the gender they identify with is if they have undergone sex-reassignment surgery.

The "Don't Ask, Don't Tell" policy is started in the United States armed forces. This was meant to allow gay military personnel to serve; prior to this they were officially forbidden from being in the armed forces. However, what it came down to was that while the military could no longer "ask" if servicepeople were gay, they were not allowed to "tell" anyone of their sexual orientation or to engage in any homosexual behavior if they wanted to continue serving.

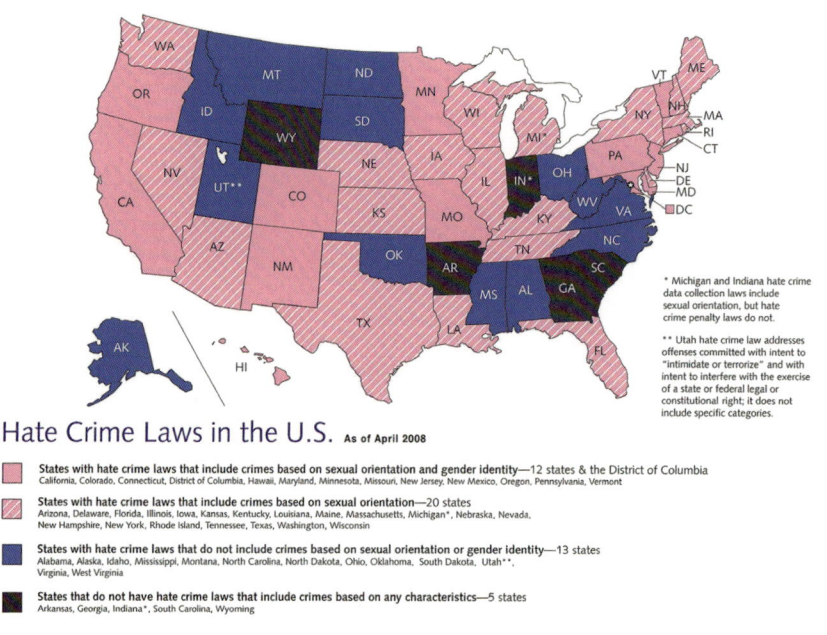

Map showing where American states stand on hate crimes, as of 2008.

78   Statistical Timeline and Overview of Gay Life

Approximately 20 percent of all persons with AIDS are found to be 20 to 29 years old; given the long *latency* period between infection and the onset of the disease, many were probably infected as teenagers.

A survey finds that 53 percent of students in Massachusetts report hearing homophobic comments made by school staff.

1996

The Federal Defense of Marriage Act (DOMA) is passed. This law defines marriage as the union between one man and one woman, at least as far as all federal laws are concerned. It also gives individual states the right not to recognize same-sex unions that have been *validated* by another state.

What's That Mean?

Latency refers to a period when a disease is active in a person's body but symptoms have not yet appeared.

Validated means being officially recognized.

1998

Matthew Shepard is murdered. Shepard was a twenty-one-year-old college student, studying political science and foreign relations at the University of Laramie,

> **What's That Mean?**
>
> A *hate crime* is a criminal act, often violent, in which the victim has been targeted because of their race, religion, or sexual orientation.

who also happened to be gay. In Laramie, Wyoming, Shepard was severely beaten and left tied to a fence post; he was eventually found by a passing cyclist over eighteen hours later and taken to the hospital, where he died a few days later. As a *hate crime*, Shepard's death became a rallying cry for organizations fighting for an end to bigotry and intolerance of all kinds.

Twenty-First Century

2000

The U.S. Census finds that at least a million children are being raised in same-sex households.

2004

Massachusetts legalizes same-sex marriage in May, while in a backlash against their actions, eleven states approved constitutional amendments that specified marriage as specifically between a man and a woman. Among these states were Arkansas, Georgia, Kentucky, Michigan, Mississippi, Montana, North Dakota, Oklahoma, Ohio, Utah, and Oregon.

Next, I'm going to read you a list of issues. Regardless of whether or not you think it should be legal, for each one, please tell me whether you personally believe that in general it is morally acceptable or morally wrong.

	Morally Acceptable	Morally Wrong
	%	%
Divorce	70	22
Gambling	63	32
The death penalty	62	30
Medical research using stem cells obtained from human embryos	62	30
Sex between an unmarried man and woman	61	36
Medical testing on animals	56	38
Having a baby outside of marriage	55	41
Buying and wearing clothing made of animal fur	54	39
Doctor assisted suicide	51	44
HOMOSEXUAL RELATIONS	48	48
Abortion	40	48
Cloning animals	33	61
Suicide	15	78
Cloning humans	11	85
Polygamy, when one husband has more than one wife at the same time	8	90
Married men and women having an affair	7	91

May 8-11, 2008

Gallup graphs on this page and the pages that follow chronicle important changes in public attitudes about homosexuality and gay rights over the past quarter century. Americans have shifted from frowning on homosexuality as an alternative lifestyle and being divided over whether it should be legal, to now supporting gay rights on both fronts. At the same time, the country remains highly ambivalent about the morality of homosexual relations, and as a result, support for legalizing gay marriage lags far behind the less culturally sensitive matter of gays having equal job rights.

James McGreevey resigns as governor of New Jersey in November. McGreevey was having an affair with a member of his staff; when he attempted to break things off, the staff member blackmailed him, threatening to go public. Instead of allowing this to happen, McGreevey told the public on his own terms, coming out as gay while admitting that his infidelity to his wife and his affair with someone on his staff was wrong. He resigned his position as governor. McGreevey went on to work as a consultant in education and policy; he divorced his wife and now lives with his new male partner.

2007

On August 9, the cable network Logo hosted a presidential debate that focused on gay issues. While all of

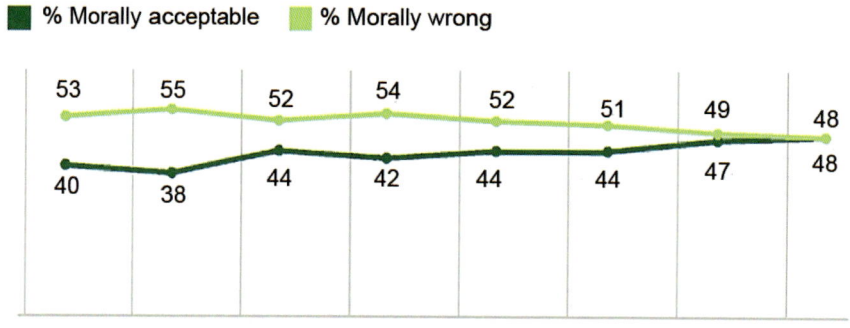

Perceptions of the Morality of Homosexual Relations

GALLUP POLL

the candidates, both Republican and Democrat were invited to participate; the Democrat candidates were the only ones who came. Participants were Hillary Clinton, John Edwards, and Barack Obama. It was sponsored by the Human Rights Campaign Foundation, as well as Logo.

In the United States, statistics estimate that nearly 255,000 men who have engaged in homosexual sex are living with HIV/AIDS, while about 5,400 have died.

2008

Both California and Connecticut pass laws that legalized same-sex marriages. However, California repeals this law the next year with the passing of Proposition 8.

On June 2, 2008, the first same-sex civil marriages in Greece take place. The mayor of the island of Tilos officiates at the marriages of two men and two women. The Greek government is still refusing to recognize these two marriages as legally valid.

2009

The Supreme Court in California upholds Proposition 8, the law that banned same-sex marriage passed in November 2008. Now, part of the state constitution reads, "Only marriage between a man and a woman is valid or recognized in California."

2010

Norrie May-Welby becomes the first person to be officially recognized as having no gender. May-Welby was born as a man, but made the transition to a woman in 1990, at age twenty-eight. However, after having gender reassignment surgery, May-Welby eventually realized that zie (zie is an ungendered pronoun used by people who define themselves as un-gendered) was not happy as a woman either. After a struggle in Australia, officials gave May-Welby a new birth certificate that certifies zer as a "neuter" individual in March 2010. However, after less than a month, May-Welby was informed that the change in gender was invalid.

On June 9, the U.S. State Department announces that transgendered individuals will no longer have to go through a sex change in order to change their gender on their passports. Up to this point, people had to prove that they had undergone gender reassignment surgery in order to be considered the gender with which they identified.

The National Gay and Lesbian Task Force concludes from its survey that 45 percent of gay males and 20 percent of lesbians surveyed have experienced verbal harassment and or physical violence during high school as a result of their sexual orientation.

In a survey of lesbians and gay men in Pennsylvania, 33 percent of gay men and 34 percent of

Do you think homosexual relations between consenting adults should or should not be legal?

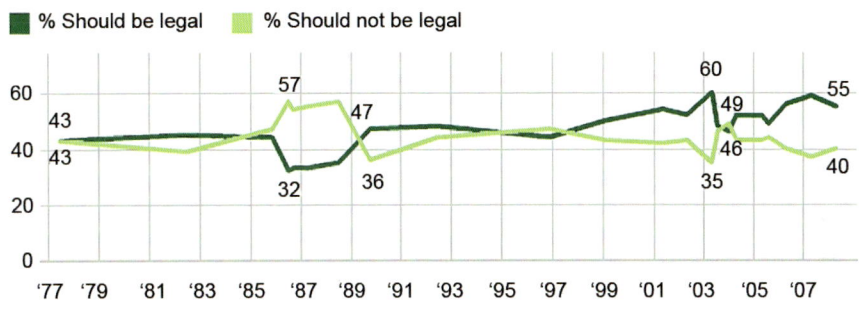

GALLUP POLL

Do you feel that homosexuality should be considered an acceptable alternative lifestyle or not?

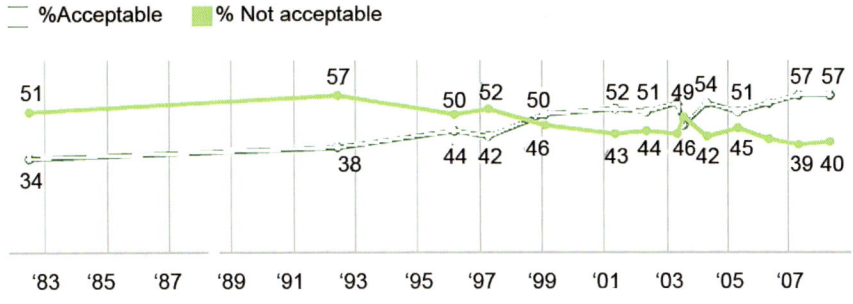

GALLUP POLL

The Modern Era 85

As you may know, there has been considerable discussion in the news regarding the rights of homosexual men and women. In general, do you think homosexuals should or should not have equal rights in terms of job opportunities?

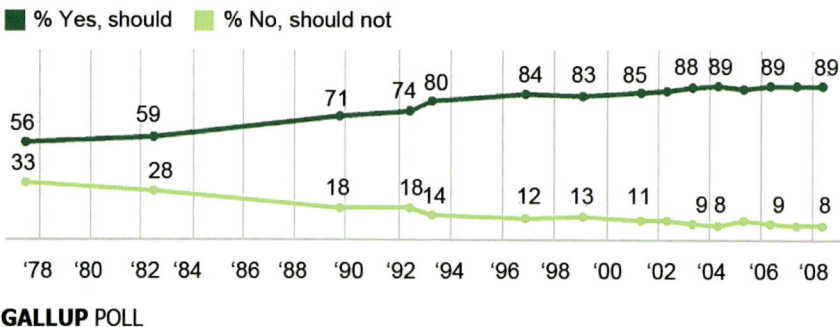

GALLUP POLL

Do you think marriages between same-sex couples should or should not be recognized by the law as valid, with the same rights as traditional marriages?

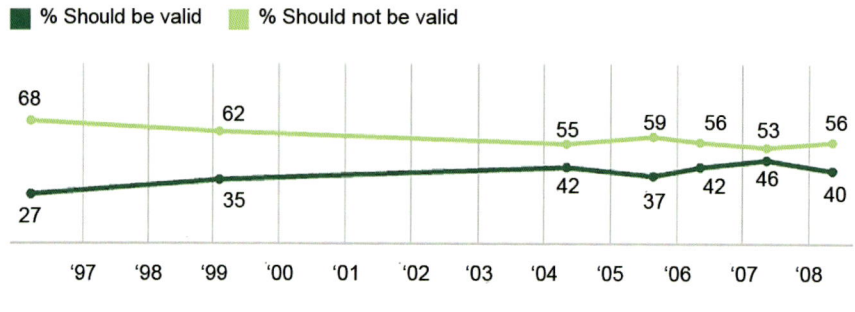

GALLUP POLL

86   Statistical Timeline and Overview of Gay Life

lesbians reported suffering physical violence at the hands of a family member as a result of their sexual orientation.

In a psychological study of 484 students at six community colleges conducted by Dr Karen Franklin, 18 percent of the men interviewed admitted that they had committed physical violence or threats against men and or women they perceived to be gay or lesbian.

BIBLIOGRAPHY

"Aquinas's Natural Law." *Internet Encyclopedia of Philosophy.* www.iep.utm.edu/sexualit/#H9 (16 June, 2010).

Archer, Bert. *The End of Gay: And the Death of Heterosexuality.* New York: Thunder's Mouth Press, 2004.

"Biographical Materials on Alfred Kinsey." The Kinsey Institute. www.kinseyinstitute.org/about/kinseybio.html (16 June 2010).

"Brazil." GlobalGayz.com, www.globalgayz.com/country/Brazil/BRA (16 June 2010).

"The Buggery Act," www.tudorplace.com.ar/Documents/the_buggery_act.htm (16 June 2010).

Chauncey, George. *Gay New York: Gender, Urban Culture, and the Making of the Gay Male World, 1890–1940.* New York: Basic Books, 1995.

"Cleveland Street Scandal." *glbtq: The World's Largest Encyclopedia of Gay, Lesbian, Bisexual, Transgendered, and Queer Culture,* www.glbtq.com/social-sciences/cleveland_street_scandal.html (16 June 2010).

"Dante Alighieri (1265–1321)." *glbtq: The World's Largest Encyclopedia of Gay, Lesbian, Bisexual, Transgendered, and Queer Culture.* www.glbtq.com/literature/dante.html (16 June 2010).

"Earl Lind." American Public University. www.spiritus-temporis.com/earl-lind/biography.html (16 June 2010).

"Elagabulus Varius Avitus Bassianus (AD 204–AD 222)." www.roman-empire.net/decline/elagabalus.html (16 June 2010).

"England & America before 1800." Gay Rights Around the World, www.gayrightssite.com/tl3.html (16 June 2010).

"English Literature: Nineteenth Century." *glbtq: The World's Largest Encyclopedia of Gay, Lesbian, Bisexual, Transgendered, and Queer Culture*, www.glbtq.com/literature/eng_lit2_19c.html (16 June 2010).

Fone, Byrne R. S. *Homophobia: A History.* New York: Metropolitan Books, 2000.

Frakes, Robert. "Why the Romans Are Important in the Debate About Gay Marriage." George Mason University's History News Network, hnn.us/articles/21319.html (16 June 2010).

"Gay Rights Movement." *History.com.* www.history.com/topics/gay-rights-movement (16 June 2010).

glbtq: The World's Largest Encyclopedia of Gay, Lesbian, Bisexual, Transgendered, and Queer Culture, www.glbtq.com/ (16 June 2010).

"Greece Sees First 'Gay Marriage.'" BBC News, June 3, 2008, news.bbc.co.uk/2/hi/7432949.stm (9 June 2010).

Guidugi, Pier Angelo. "Who's On First? The Last Execution for Homosexuality in the West." South Florida Gay News.com (16 June 2010).

"Harvey Milk." *Encyclopedia of World Biography*, www.notablebiographies.com/Ma-Mo/Milk-Harvey.html (10 June 2010).

"History of AIDS up to 1986." AVERT: AVERTing HIV and AIDS, May 13, 2010, www.avert.org/aids-history-86.htm (10 June 2010).

"History of Homosexuality." Buzzle.com: Intelligent Life on the Web, www.buzzle.com/editorials/7-17-2004-56743.asp (16 June 2010).

"HIV, AIDS, and Young Gay Men." AVERT: AVERTing HIV and AIDS, February 19, 2010, www.avert.org/young-gay-men.htm (9 June 2010).

Holland, William. "Mwah . . . Is this the First Recorded Gay Kiss?: Egyptian Manicurists Become Homosexual Icons." *The Sunday Times,* January 1, 2006 www.timesonline.co.uk/tol/news/uk/article784046.ece (9 June 2010).

"Homosexual." *Online Etymological Dictionary*. www.etymonline.com/index.php?search = homosexual&searchmode = none (16 June 2010).

Hughes, Glyn. "The Condensed Edition of Plato of Athens' *The Symposium* . . . in Just 2600 Words." Glyn Hughes' Squashed Philosophers, www.btinternet.com/ ~ glynhughes/squashed/plato-symposium.htm (9 June 2010).

"Inquisition." *glbtq: The World's Largest Encyclopedia of Gay, Lesbian, Bisexual, Transgendered, and Queer Culture*, www.glbtq.com/social-sciences/inquisition.html (16 June 2010).

Johnson, Ryan D. "Homosexuality: Nature or Nurture?" AllPsych Online: The Virtual Psychology Classroom, April 30, 2003, allpsych.com/journal/homosexuality.html (10 June 2010).

Johnson, Ted. "Dems Debate Gay Issues on Logo: Etheidge Poses Questions to Clinton, Obama." *Variety,* July 10, 2007, www.variety.com/article/VR1117968321.html?categoryid = 14&cs = 1 (9 June 2010).

"Joseph and His Friend: A Story of Pennsylvania." WorldLingo, www.worldlingo.com/ma/enwiki/en/Joseph_and_His_Friend:_A_Story_of_Pennsylvania#cite_note-2 (16 June 2010).

"Karl Heinrich Ulrichs." StoneWall Society, www.stonewallsociety.com/famouspeople/karl.htm (16 June 2010).

Koymasky, Matt and Andrej. "The Gay Holocaust—Memorials." The Memorial Hall, June 30, 2008, andrejkoymasky.com/mem/holocaust/ho08.html (10 June 2010).

Matthew Shepard Foundation, www.matthewshepard.org/site/PageServer?pagename = Our_Story_Main_Page (9 June 2010).

May, Norrie. "I Who May Well Be. . . ," may-welby.blogspot.com/ (9 June 2010).

McGreevey, James E. "The Making of a Gay American." *New York Magazine*, September 18, 2006, nymag.com/news/politics/21340/ (9 June 2010).

Melville, Raymond. "Dr. Magnus Hirschfeld." StoneWall Society, www.stonewallsociety.com/famouspeople/magnus.htm (16 June 2010).

Miller, Neil. *Out of the Past: Gay and Lesbian History from 1869 to the Present*. New York: Vintage Books, 1996.

"Napoleonic Code." *glbtq: The World's Largest Encyclopedia of Gay, Lesbian, Bisexual, Transgendered, and Queer Culture,* www.glbtq.com/social-sciences/napoleonic_code.html (16 June 2010).

North, Alix. "Sappho, circa 630 BCE." The Isle of Lesbos, www.sappho.com/poetry/sappho.html (9 June 2010).

Norton, Rictor. "A History of Homophobia: 3 The Later Roman Empire & The Early Middle Ages." rictornorton.co.uk/homopho3.htm (16 June 2010).

Norton, Rictor. "The Trial of Richard Cornish 1624." Homosexuality in Eighteenth-Century England, rictornorton.co.uk/eighteen/cornish.htm (16 June 2010).

"The Notebooks of Leonardo da Vinci." Read Easily: Ebooks Online Library, www.readeasily.com/leonardo-da-vinci/index.php (16 June 2010).

"Oscar Wilde's Trial." eSSORTMENT. www.essortment.com/all/oscarwildeplay_rghw.htm (16 June 2010).

"Oscar Wilde's Trial—The Crime of Homosexuality." Suite101.com, victorian-fiction.suite101.com/article.cfm/oscar_wildes_trial_the_crime_of_homosexuality (16 June 2010).

Painter, George. "The History of Sodomy Laws in the United States: Connecticut." Sodomy Laws, www.glapn.org/sodomylaws/sensibilities/connecticut.htm (16 June 2010).

Painter, George. "The History of Sodomy Laws in the United States: Virginia." Sodomy Laws, www.glapn.org/sodomylaws/sensibilities/virginia.htm (16 June 2010).

Percy, William Armstrong III. *Pederasty and Pedagogy in Archaic Greece.* Champaign-Urbana: University of Illinois Press, 1996.

Peterson, Kavan. "50-State Rundown on Gay Marriage Laws." Stateline.org, November 3, 2004, www.stateline.org/live/ViewPage.action?siteNodeId = 136&languageId = 1&contentId = 15576 (9 June 2010).

Ramsland, Katherine. "Teena Brandon." TruTV, www.trutv.com/library/crime/notorious_murders/not_guilty/brandon/1.html (10 June 2010).

"The Richard Cornish Endowment Fund." William and Mary Gay and Lesbian Alumni, Inc., wmgala.wordpress.com/about/cornish-fund/ (16 June 2010).

"Russian Gay History." community.middlebury.edu/~moss/RGC2.html (16 June 2010).

"Sacred Band of Thebes." www.mlahanas.de/Greeks/History/SacredBandOfThebes.html (16 June 2010).

"Surgery No Longer a Requirement for Changing Gender on Passport." CNN, June 9, 2010, www.cnn.com/2010/US/06/09/passports.transgender/ (10 June 2010).

Thompson, Mark. "'Don't Ask, Don't Tell' Turns 15." *Time*, January 28, 2008, www.time.com/time/nation/article/0,8599,1707545,00.html (10 June 2010).

What is Prop 8? www.whatisprop8.com/ (9 June 2010).

INDEX

Africa 11
AIDS 68–69, 71, 79, 83
American Psychiatric Association (APA) 59, 64
Aquinas, Thomas 22

bisexual 42, 54–55, 72–73
Brazil 36–37
Buchanan, James 37

Catholic Church 61, 64
Christianity 10, 20–22, 49
civil rights 56
Cleveland Street Scandal 40
Constantine 20
cross-dressing 33

da Vinci, Leonardo 23–24
Denmark 52, 72–73
depression 73–74
discrimination 9, 20, 36–37, 67, 78
Divine Comedy 22
"Don't Ask, Don't Tell" 78

Egypt 10
execution 26, 28, 39

"faggot" 47
Federal Defense of Marriage Act (DOMA) 79
First Amendment 60

gay pride 63–64, 72

Germany 39, 44, 46, 54, 56
Goldman, Emma 46–47

Hall, Radclyffe 49–50
harassment 72–73, 84
hate crime 72, 78, 80
Henry VIII 26–27
Hirschfeld, Magnus 44–45, 52
Holocaust 70–71
homoerotic 12, 25
Hooker, Evelyn 59

Inquisition 26, 28

Jefferson, Thomas 34–35
Julius Bar 62

Kinsey, Alfred 41–43

Lavender Scare 56
Laws of Manu 19
Leaves of Grass 39

Mattachine Society, The 56, 62–63
May-Welby, Norrie 84
McCarthy, Joseph 56–57
Milk, Harvey 66–68
Mormon 64

National Gay and Lesbian Task Force 84
Nazi Party 44, 51–52, 54, 56
Nero 19
New Haven 31

Obama, Barack 83
Officers of the Night Court 25

pederasty 14–15
Persia 25
Plato 14
Proposition 8 83
prostitute 23, 40

rainbow flag 66–67
Renaissance 23, 25
Roman Empire 19–20
Russia 37, 46, 48, 52

sacrament 20
Sacred Band of Thebes 18
San Francisco 62, 64, 66–67, 75–76
Sappho 11–13
sexual orientation 6–7, 56, 67, 72, 77, 79–80, 84, 87

Shepard, Matthew 79–80
sodomy 22–23, 26, 28, 31, 34–36, 39, 43–44, 62, 64
Soviet Union 37, 48, 52
Stonewall riots 62–64, 68
suicide 71, 73
Symposium 14, 18

Teena, Brandon 77
Thailand 16, 59
Two-Spirit individuals 15

Ulrichs, Karl 39

Veterans Benevolent Association (VBA) 54–55
Vice Versa 55

Whitman, Walt 39
Wilde, Oscar 42–43

Index 95

ABOUT THE AUTHOR AND THE CONSULTANT

Zachary Chastain is an editor and staff writer at Harding House Publishing Service, where he has worked for the past four years. Other editors and writers at Harding House also helped him research and compile this timeline of LGBT history, including Emily Sanna, Kim Etingoff, Camden Flath, and William Palmer.

James T. Sears specializes in research in lesbian, gay, bisexual, and transgender issues in education, curriculum studies, and queer history. His scholarship has appeared in a variety of peer-reviewed journals and he is the author or editor of twenty books and is the Editor of the *Journal of LGBT Youth*. Dr. Sears has taught curriculum, research, and LGBT-themed courses in the departments of education, sociology, women's studies, and the honors college at several universities, including: Trinity University, Indiana University, Harvard University, Penn State University, the College of Charleston, and the University of South Carolina. He has also been a Research Fellow at Center for Feminist Studies at the University of Southern California, a Fulbright Senior Research Southeast Asia Scholar on sexuality and culture, a Research Fellow at the University of Queensland, a consultant for the J. Paul Getty Center for Education and the Arts, and a Visiting Research Lecturer in Brazil. He lectures throughout the world.